A CHIP IN
THE SUGAR

A Monologue from *Talking Heads*

by Alan Bennett

samuelfrench.co.uk

FOR AMATEUR PRODUCTION ENQUIRIES

UNITED KINGDOM AND WORLD
EXCLUDING NORTH AMERICA
plays@samuelfrench.co.uk
020 7255 4302/01

Each title is subject to availability from Samuel French,
depending upon country of performance.

THINKING ABOUT PERFORMING A SHOW?

There are thousands of plays and musicals available to perform from Samuel French right now, and applying for a licence is easier and more affordable than you might think

From classic plays to brand new musicals, from monologues to epic dramas, there are shows for everyone.

Plays and musicals are protected by copyright law so if you want to perform them, the first thing you'll need is a licence. This simple process helps support the playwright by ensuring they get paid for their work, and means that you'll have the documents you need to stage the show in public.

Not all our shows are available to perform all the time, so it's important to check and apply for a licence before you start rehearsals or commit to doing the show.

LEARN MORE & FIND THOUSANDS OF SHOWS

Browse our full range of plays and musicals and find out more about how to license a show
www.samuelfrench.co.uk/perform

Talk to the friendly experts in our Licensing team for advice on choosing a show, and help with licensing
plays@samuelfrench.co.uk   020 7387 9373

Acting Editions

BORN TO PERFORM

Playscripts designed from the ground up to work the way you do in rehearsal, performance and study

---

Larger, clearer text for easier reading

Wider margins for notes

Performance features such as character and props lists, sound and lighting cues, and more

---

+ CHOOSE A SIZE AND STYLE TO SUIT YOU

STANDARD EDITION

Our regular paperback book at our regular size

SPIRAL-BOUND EDITION

The same size as the Standard Edition, but with a sturdy, easy-to-fold, easy-to-hold spiral-bound spine

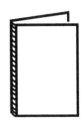

LARGE EDITION

A4 size and spiral bound, with larger text and a blank page for notes opposite every page of text. Perfect for technical and directing use

---

LEARN MORE   **samuelfrench.co.uk/actingeditions**

Other plays by ALAN BENNETT
published and licensed by Samuel French

Bed Among the Lentils

A Cream Cracker Under the Settee

Enjoy

Getting On

Habeas Corpus

Her Big Chance

Kafka's Dick

A Lady of Letters

Office Suite: Green Forms & A Visit from Miss Prothero

The Old Country

Say Something Happened

Single Spies

Soldiering On

The Wind in the Willows

The Wind in the Willows (songbook)

A Woman of No Importance

ABOUT THE AUTHOR

Alan Bennett was born in Leeds in 1934. After studying at Oxford University he collaborated as a writer and performer with Dudley Moore, Jonathan Miller and Peter Cook in *Beyond the Fringe* in 1960 at the Edinburgh Festival.

He then turned to writing full time and produced his first stage play *Forty Years On* in 1968. His other plays include *Getting On, Habeas Corpus, The Old Country, The Lady in the Van, A Question of Attribution, The Madness of George III* (together with the Oscar-nominated screenplay *The Madness of King George*), an adaptation of Kenneth Grahame's *The Wind in the Willows* and *The History Boys*; as well as many television plays such as *A Day Out, Sunset across the Bay, A Woman of No Importance* and the series of monologues *Talking Heads* and *Talking Heads II.*

AUTHOR'S NOTE

"I didn't say anything": this is the phrase most often uttered by Graham, a middle-aged bachelor, in this acute study of a lonely and repressed life from Alan Bennett's *Talking Heads* series. Emotionally retarded and chronically dependent on his mother, with whom he lives, Graham finds life difficult enough at the best of times; when Mother meets an old flame and seems set to marry him, however, Graham's old insecurities (Will he be parted from his mother? Is there someone watching the house?) rear their ugly heads again. Fate, eventually, rescues Graham and he resumes his normal life of banal muddle under his mother's amnesiac tyranny. This monologue represents Graham's obsessive outpourings, which are touching, amusing, and disturbing simultaneously and provide a major challenge for the actor.

Scenery
No attempt should be made to make the setting realistic. There should be no unnecessary decoration, and no furniture additional to that needed in the action.

Lighting
In order to avoid applause, the lights should fade between each section of the play, as indicated, but not to black-out, the only black-out being at the end of the play. The performer should be visible in the fade as sometimes there is relevant action between the scenes.

A CHIP IN THE SUGAR

First shown on BBC TV on 19 April 1988. The cast was as follows:

GRAHAM   Alan Bennett

Directed by Stuart Burge
Produced by Innes Lloyd
Designed by Tony Burrough

Subsequently performed as part of the stage version of *Talking Heads*, which opened on 28 January 1992. The cast was as follows:

GRAHAM   Alan Bennett

Directed by Alan Bennett
Designed by Simon Higlett

GRAHAM*'s bedroom.*

There is a bed, covered with a dull bedspread, a bedside table with a cup of tea on it, and a wardrobe. There are upright chairs downstage right and downstage left and a high armchair right. The walls are papered in a plain, dull fashion.

Music plays; as the curtain rises it fades.

GRAHAM, *a mild middle-aged man, sits in the armchair right.*

GRAHAM I'd just taken her tea up this morning when she said, "Graham, I think the world of you." I said, "I think the world of you." And she said, "That's all right then." I said, "What's brought this on?" She said, "Nothing. This tea looks strong, pull the curtains." Of course I knew what had brought it on. She said, "I wouldn't like you to think you're not Number One." So I said, "Well, you're Number One with me too. Give me your teeth. I'll swill them."

What it was we'd had a spot of excitement yesterday: we ran into a bit of Mother's past. I said to her, "I didn't know you had a past. I thought I was your past." She said, "You?" I said, "Well, we go back a long way. How does he fit in *vis-à-vis* Dad?" She laughed. "Oh, he was pre-Dad." I said, "Pre-Dad? I'm surprised you remember him, you don't remember to switch your blanket off."

She said, "That's different. His name's Turnbull." I said, "I know. He said."

I'd parked her by the war memorial on her usual seat while I went and got some reading matter. Then I waited while she went and spent a penny in the disabled toilet. She's not actually disabled, her memory's bad, but she says she prefers their toilets because you get more elbow room. She always takes forever, diddling her hands and what not, and when she eventually comes back it turns out she's been chatting to the attendant. I said, "What about?" She said, "Hanging." She was in favour of stiffer penalties for minor offences and I thought, "Well, we know better, our Graham and me." I wish you'd been there, love; you could have given her the statistics, where are we going for our tea?'

The thing about Mam is that though she's never had a proper education, she's picked up enough from me to be able to hold her own in discussions about up-to-the-minute issues like the environment and the colour problem, and for a woman of her age and background she has a very liberal slant. She'll look at my *Guardian* and she actually thinks for herself. Doctor Chaudhury said to me, "Full marks, Graham. The best way to avoid a broken hip is to have a flexible mind. Keep up the good work."

They go mad round the war memorial so when we cross over I'll generally slip my arm through hers until we're safely across, only once we're on the pavement she'll postpone letting it go, because once upon a time we got stopped by one of these questionnaire women who reckons to take us for husband and wife. I mean, Mam's got white hair. She was doing this dodge and I said, "Mam, let go of my arm." I didn't really wrench it, only next thing I know she's flat on the pavement. I said, "Oh my God, Mother."

People gather round and I pick up her bag, and she sits up and says, "I've laddered both my stockings." I said, "Never mind your stockings, what about your pelvis?" She says, "It's these bifocals. They tell you not to look down. I was avoiding some sick." Somebody says, "That's a familiar voice," and there's a little fellow bending over her, green trilby hat, shorty raincoat. "Hallo," he says, "remember me?"

Well, she doesn't remember people, I know for a fact because she swore me down she'd never met Joy Buckle, who teaches

Rowers in Felt and Fabric at my day centre. I said, "You have met Joy, you knitted her a tea-cosy." That's all she can knit, tea cosies. And bed socks. Both outmoded articles. I said to her, "Branch out. If you can knit tea cosies you can knit skiing hats." She says, "Well, I will." Only I have to stand over her or else she'll still leave a hole for the spout. "Anyway," I said, "you do remember Joy because you said she had some shocking eyebrows." She said, "Well, I don't remember." And that's the way she is, she doesn't remember and here's this little fellow saying, "Do you remember me?" So I said, "No she won't. Come on, Mother. Let's get you up." Only she says, "Remember you? Of course. It's Frank Turnbull. It must be fifty years." He said, "Fifty-three. Filey. 1938." She said, "Sea-Crest." He said, "No sand in the bedrooms." And they both cracked out laughing.

Meanwhile she's still stuck on the cold pavement. I said, "Come along, Mother. We don't want piles." Only he butts in again. He says, "With respect, it's advisable not to move a person until it's been ascertained no bones are broken. I was in the St John's Ambulance Brigade." "Yes," said Mother, "and who did you learn your bandaging on?" And they both burst out laughing again. He had on these bright yellow gloves, could have been a bookie.

Eventually, I get my arms round her waist and hoist her up, only his lordship's no help as he claims to have a bad back. When I've finally got her restored to the perpendicular she introduces him. "This is Frank Turnbull, a friend of mine from the old days." What old days? First time I knew there were any old days. Turns out he's a gents' outfitter, semi-retired, shop in Bradford and some sort of outlet in Morecambe. I thought, "Well, that accounts for the yellow gloves."

Straight off he takes charge. He says, "What you need now, Vera, is a cup of coffee." I said, "Well, we were just going for some tea, weren't we, Mother?" Vera! Her name's not Vera. She's never been called Vera. My dad never called her

Vera, except just once, when they were wheeling him into the theatre. Vera. "Right," he says, "follow me." And puts his arm through hers. "Careful," she says. "You'll make my boyfriend jealous." I didn't say anything.

Pause.

Now the café we generally patronize is just that bit different. It's plain but it's classy, no cloths on the tables, the menu comes on a little slate and the waitresses wear their own clothes and look as if they're doing it just for the fun of it. The stuff's all homemade and we're both big fans of the date and walnut bread. I said, "This is the place." Mr Turnbull goes straight past. "No," he says, "I know somewhere, just opened. Press on."

Now, if there's one thing Mother and me are agreed on it's that red is a common colour. And the whole place is done out in red. Lampshades red. Waitresses in red. Plates red, and on the tables those plastic sauce dispenser things got up to look like tomatoes. Also red. And when I look there's a chip in the sugar. I thought, "Mother won't like this." "Oh," she says, "this looks cheerful, doesn't it, Graham?" I said, "There's a chip in the sugar." "A detail," he says, "they're still having their teething troubles. Is it three coffees?" I said, "We like tea," only Mother says, "No. I feel like a change. I'll have coffee." He gets hold of the menu and puts his hand on hers. "Might I advise," he says, "a cheeseburger?" She said, "Oh, what's that?" He said, "It's fresh country beef, mingled with golden-fried onions, topped off with toasted cheese served with french fries and lemon wedge." "Oh, lemon wedge," she says. "That sounds nice." I thought, "Well, I hope you can keep it down." Because it'll be the pizza saga all over again. One mouthful and at four o'clock in the morning I was still stuck at her bedside with the bucket. She said, "I like new experiences in eating. I had a pizza once, didn't I, Graham?" I didn't say anything.

They fetch the food and she's wiring in. He said, "Are you enjoying your cheeseburger?" She said, "I am. Would I be mistaken in thinking that receptacle contains tomato sauce?" He said, "It is." She says, "Give us a squirt." They both burst out laughing. He said, "Glass cups, Graham. Be careful or we'll see up your nose." More laughter. She said, "Graham's quite refined. He often has a dry sherry."

"Well, he could do with smartening up a bit," Mr Turnbull said. "Plastic mac. He wants one of these quilted jobs, I've shifted a lot of those." "I don't like those quilted jobs," I said. "He sweats," Mother said. "There's no excuse for that in this day and age," Mr Turnbull said, "the range of preparations there are on the market. You want to invest in some roll-on deodorant." Everybody could hear. "And flares are anathema even in Bradford."

"Graham doesn't care, do you, Graham?" Mother said. "He reads a lot." "So what?" Mr Turnbull said. "I know several big readers who still manage to be men about town. Lovat green's a nice shade. I tell you this, Graham," he said, "if I were squiring a young lady like this around town I wouldn't do it in grey socks and sandals. These shoes are Italian. Feel." "I always think Graham would have made a good parson," Mother said, feeling his foot, "only he doesn't believe in God." "That's no handicap these days," Mr Turnbull said. "What do you do?"

"He's between jobs at present," Mother said. "He used to do soft toys for handicapped children. Then he was making paper flowers at one stage." I went to the toilet.

Pause.

When I came back he said, "I don't believe in mental illness. Nine times out of ten it's a case of pulling your socks up." I didn't say anything. Mother said, "Yes, well, I think the pendulum's gone too far." She didn't look at me. "It's like these girls, not eating," he said, "they'd eat if they'd been brought up like us, Vera, nothing to eat." "That's right," Mother said, "they have it too easy. Did you marry?" "Twice," he said. "I buried Amy last May. I was heartbroken but life has to go on. I've a son lives in Stevenage. I've got two grandsons, one at the motorbike stage. Do you drive?" "No," I said. "You do," Mother said. "You had that scooter." "It was only a moped," I said. "Well, a moped, Graham. They're all the same. I can't get him to blow his own trumpet."

"I've got a Rover two thousand," Mr Turnbull said, "handles like a dream. I think the solution to mental illness is hard physical work. Making raffia mats, I'd go mad." "Yes," says Mother, "only they do pottery as well. I've seen some nice ashtrays." "Featherbedding," Mr Turnbull said. "Do you like these Pakistanis?" "Well, in moderation," Mother said. "We have a nice newsagent. Graham thinks we're all the same." I said, "I thought you did." She said, "Well, I do when you explain it all to me, Graham, but then I forget the explanation and I'm back to square one." "There is no explanation," Mr Turnbull said. "They sell mangoes in our post office, what explanation is there for that?" "I know," Mother said, "I smelled curry on my *Woman's Own*. You have to be educated to understand." I didn't say anything.

He ran us home, promised to give her a tinkle next time he was in the neighbourhood. Said he was often round here tracking down two-tone cardigans. "Your mother's a grand woman," he said. "You want to cherish her." "He does, he does," Mother said. "You're my boyfriend, aren't you, Graham?" She put her arm through mine.

Music plays and the lights fade, but not to complete darkness; GRAHAM *is visible as he moves to stand down stage of the downstage right chair.*

The music fades and the lights return to normal.

There must be a famine on somewhere because we were just letting our midday meal go down when the vicar calls with some envelopes. Breezes in, anorak and running shoes, and he says, "I always look forward to coming to this house, Mrs Whittaker." (He's got the idea she's deaf, which she's not; it's one of the few things she isn't.) He says, "Do you know why? It's because you two remind me of Jesus and his mother." Well, I've always thought Jesus was a bit off-hand with his mother, and on one occasion I remember he was quite snotty with her, but I didn't say anything. And of course Madam is over the moon. In her book if you can't get compared with the Queen Mother the Virgin Mary's the next best thing. She says, "Are you married?" (She asks him every time, never remembers.) He said, "No, Mrs Whittaker. I am married to God." She says, "Where does that leave you with the housework?" He said, "Well, I don't do as well as your Graham. He's got this place like a palace." She says, "Well, I do my whack. I washed four pairs of stockings this morning." She hadn't. She put them in the bowl then they slipped her mind, so the rest of the operation devolved on me.

He moves to the armchair and sits.

He said, "How are you today, Mrs Whittaker?" She says, "Stiff down one side." I said, "She had a fall yesterday." She says, "I never did." I said, "You did, Mother. You had a fall, then you ran into Mr Turnbull."

Pause.

She says, "That's right. I did." And she starts rooting in her bag for her lipstick. She says, "That's one of them anoraky things, isn't it? They've gone out now, those. If you want to look like a man about town you want to get one of those continental quilts." He said, "Oh?" I said, "She means them quilted jackets." She said, "He knows what I mean. Where did you get those shoes?" He said, "They're training shoes." She said, "Training for what? Are you not fully qualified?" He said, "If Jesus were alive today, Mrs Whittaker, I think you'd find these were the type of shoes he would be wearing." "Not if his mother had anything to do with it," she said. "She'd have him down Stead and Simpson's and get him into some good brogues. Somebody was telling me the Italians make good shoes."

The vicar takes this as his cue to start on about people who have no shoes at all and via this to the famine in Ethiopia. I fork out fifty p which he says will feed six families for a week and she says, "Well, it would have bought me some Quality Street." When he's at the door he says, "I take my hat off to you, Graham, I've got a mother of my own." When I get back in she said, "Vicar! He looked more like the paperboy. How can you look up to somebody in pumps?" Just then there's a knock at the door. "Get down," she says, "he's back."

He rises and moves center.

Only it isn't. It's Mr Turnbull.

New outfit this time: little suede coat, corduroy collar, maroon trousers. She says, "You're colourful." "We just happen to have these slacks on offer," he says. "I was wondering whether you fancied a run out to Bolton Abbey?" "Bolton Abbey?" she says. "Oh, that's right up our street, isn't it, Graham? Graham's good with buildings, aren't you, Graham? He knows all the periods of houses. There's one period that's just come in. Other people don't like it yet but we do, don't we, Graham?" "I don't know," I said. "You do. What is it?" "Victorian," I said. "That's it, Victorian. Only there's a lot been pulled down." Mr Turnbull yawns. "I've got a little bungalow." "That's nice," Mother says. "I like a nice bungalow, don't you, Graham?" "Yes," I said, "provided it's not a blot on the landscape." "Mine's architect designed," says Mr Turnbull. "It has a patio and a breakfast bar, it overlooks a beauty spot." "Oh," said Mother, "sounds tip-top. We'd better be getting our skates on, Graham." He said, "I've got to pick up a load of green three-quarter-length windcheaters in Ilkley; there won't really be room for a third party. Isn't there anything on at the pictures?" "Oh he'll be happy reading," Mother said. "Won't you, Graham?" "Anyway," Mr Turnbull said, "you don't always want to be with your Mother at your age, do you, Graham?" I didn't say anything.

He moves downstage of the right chair.

I've been laid on my bed reading. I've a feeling that somebody's looking at the house, only I can't see anybody. Once or twice I think I've heard a knock on the door, but I haven't gone in case there's nobody there.

Music plays.

He looks downstage left, where the window is imagined to be, then sits in the chair right.

The lights fade, then rise again on GRAHAM *sitting in the same position.*

The music fades.

Today they went over to York. It was after seven when he dropped her off. He generally comes in but not this time. Just gives her a little kiss. She has to bend down. I said, "Have you had a good time?" She said, "Yes. We had egg and chips, tea, bread and butter, we've got a lot in common and there's a grand new car park." I said, "Did you go in the Minster?" She said, "No. Frank's not keen on old buildings. We need to look more to the future. He says they've built a spanking new precinct in Bradford, so that's going to be next on the agenda. You're quiet." I said, "Well, do you wonder? Doctor Chaudhury says I should have a stable environment. This isn't a stable environment with your fancy men popping in every five minutes." She said, "He isn't my fancy man." I said, "Well, he's your fancy man in embryo." She said, "You know I don't know what that means." I said, "How old are you?" She said, "I don't know." I said, "You do know." She said, "I don't. Tell me." I said, "You're seventy-two." "That's not so old. How old was Winston Churchill?" I said, "When?" She said, "You think you've got it over me, Graham Whittaker. Well, I'll tell you something, my memory's better with Frank. He was telling me about the economy. You've got it all wrong." I said, "How?" "I can't remember but you have. Blaming it on the government. Frank says it's the blacks."

He rises and moves to the left of the downstage left chair.

I didn't say anything, just came upstairs.

When I went down again she's still sat there with her hat and coat on. I said: "Do you want to knit him a tea-cosy?" She said, "No, I don't think he's the tea-cosy type. When I first met him he had a motorbike and sidecar. Besides, I think it's got beyond the tea-cosy stage." I said, "What do you mean?" She said, "Graham. My one aim in life is for you to be happy. If I thought that by dying I could make you happy I would." I said, "Mother, your dying wouldn't make me happy. It would make me unhappy. Anyway, Mother, you're not going to die." She said, "No. I'm not going to die. I'm going to get married. And the honeymoon is in Tenerife. Have one of your tablets."

He sits in the armchair.

She made a cup of tea. I said, "How can you go to Tenerife, you were smothered at Scarborough?" She said, "It's a four-star hotel with tip-top air-conditioning, you get your breakfast from a long table." I said, "What about your bowels?" She said, "What about my bowels?" "Well, you said they were unpredictable at Morecambe. Get them to the Canary Islands and they're going to be all over the place." She said, "Who's talking about the Canary Islands? I'm going to Tenerife." "And what about post-Tenerife? Where are you going to live?" She said, "Here. Frank says he'll be away on and off on business but he wants to call this home." I said, "What about me?" She went into the kitchen. "Well, we wondered whether you'd prefer to go back to the hostel. You were happy at the hostel. You rubbed shoulders with all sorts." I said, "Mam. This is my home." She said:

He stands.

"A man shouldn't be living with his mother at your age, Frank says. Did you take a tablet?"

He moves right of the armchair, looking nervously left, out of the window.

Now it's four o'clock in the morning and I can't sleep. There's a car parked outside. I can't see but I think there's somebody in it, watching like they used to do before. I thought all that chapter was closed.

Music plays and the lights fade, but not to complete darkness. GRAHAM *moves to the bedside table and picks up the cup of tea. Then, gazing out of the window downstage left, he moves to the left chair, sits and drinks.*

The music fades and the lights return to normal.

This morning I went to Community Caring down at the Health Centre. It caters for all sorts. Steve, who runs it, is dead against what he calls "the ghetto approach". What he's after is a nice mix of personality difficulties as being the most fruitful exercise in problem-solving and a more realistic model of society generally. There's a constant flow of coffee, "oiling the wheels" Steve calls it, and we're all encouraged to ventilate our problems and generally let our hair down. I sometimes feel a bit out of it as I've never had any particular problems, so this time when Steve says, "Now chaps and chappesses, who's going to set the ball rolling?" I get in quick and tell them about Mother and Mr Turnbull. When I'd finished Steve said, "Thank you, Graham, for sharing your problem with us. Does anybody want to kick it around?"

First off the mark is Leonard, who wonders whether Graham has sufficiently appreciated that old people can fall in love and have meaningful relationships generally, the same as young people. I suppose this is understandable coming from Leonard because he's sixty-five, only he doesn't have meaningful relationships. He's been had up for exposing himself in Sainsbury's doorway. As Mother said, "Tesco, you could understand it."

Then Janice chips in. "Had they been having sexual inter-course?" I said I didn't want to think about it. Steve said, "Why?" I said I didn't know. So he said, "Maybe what we should be talking about is why Graham is being so defensive about sexual intercourse." I said, "Steve. I am not being defensive about sexual intercourse. She is my mother." Jackie, who's nine parts lesbian, said, "Graham. She is also A Woman." I couldn't believe this. I said, "Jackie. You're an ex-battered wife. I thought you didn't approve of marriage." She said, "Graham. I approve of caring marriage." I said, "Jackie. This is not caring marriage." She said, "Graham, what's Tenerife? That's caring. All I got was a black eye and a day trip to Fleetwood." Then they all have a go. Get Graham. Steve sums up. "The general feeling of the group is that Graham could be more open." I said, "How can I be more open? There's somebody sat outside the house watching." I wanted to discuss that only Leonard leaped in and said he felt the need to talk through an episode behind British Home Stores. I stuck it a bit longer and then came home.

Mother's sat there, all dolled up. Earrings on, chiffon scarf, lathered in make-up. She said, "Oh, I thought you were Mr Turnbull." I said, "No." She said, "I'll just go to the lav." She goes three times in the next ten minutes. I said, "You're not getting married today, are you?" She said, "No. There's a new Asda superstore opened at Bingley and we thought we'd give it the once over. Frank says they have a very good selection of sun tan lotions." I said, "Mother, there's somebody watching the house." She said, "I want to pick out some tissues and Frank's looking for a little chammy for his windscreen. He's promised me something called a cheeseburger, there's a café that's part of the complex.'

Just then there's a little toot on the horn and she runs to the lav again. I said, "Don't go."

He rises and moves right of the armchair.

"Don't leave me, Mam." She said, "I'm not giving in to you, you're a grown man. Is my underskirt showing?" He toots again.

He moves left of the armchair.

She says, "Look at your magazines, make yourself a poached egg." I said, "Mam." She said, "There's that bit of chicken in the fridge. You could iron those two vests. Take a tablet Give us a kiss. Toodle pip."

He backs upstage and sits on the edge of the bed.

I thought I'd go sit in the back room where they couldn't see me. I pulled the curtains and I'm sitting there in the dark and I think I hear a knock at the front door. I don't move and there's another knock. Louder. I do like Doctor Chaudhury says and tell myself it's not happening, only it is. Somebody shouts through the letter-box. "I know you're in there. Open this door."

He moves downstage.

So I do. And there *is* someone. It's a woman.

She said, "Are you the son?" I said, "What?" She said, "Are you the son? I'm the daughter." I said, "Have you been watching the house?" She said, "On and off. Why?" I said, "Nothing." She said, "I don't know what there is to look so suited about." I said, "You'd better come in."

He moves to the right of the wardrobe.

The lights fade, **GRAHAM** *moves to the armchair and sits.*

The lights return to normal.

It's nine o'clock when I hear the car outside. I'm sitting watching TV. I say, "Oh hallo. Did you have a nice time?" She said, "Yes. Yes we did, thank you." "Did you get your sun tan lotion?" She said, "What sun tan lotion?" "You were going to get some sun tan lotion. Never mind. You've forgotten. How's Mr Turnbull?" "Frank? He's all right." She took her things off. "I'm sure you could get to like him, Graham, if only you got to know him." I said, "Well, you should have brought him in." "Well, I will next time. It'd be nice if now and again we could go off as a threesome. What have you done?" "Nothing," I said. "Just sat here." "You've been all right?" "Mmm."

"You see," she said, "there wasn't anybody outside." "Oh yes there was." She said, "Oh Graham. Have you had a tablet? Have a tablet." "I don't want a tablet. I'll tell you who was sat outside. Mrs Pamela Musgrave." She said, "Who's she?" "Née Turnbull. The daughter of your hubby to be." She said, "He hasn't got a daughter. He's got a son down south. He hasn't got a daughter," she said, "you're making stuff up now, have a tablet." I said, "I'm not making it up. And there's something else I'm not making up. Mrs Turnbull." She said, "There isn't a Mrs Turnbull. She's dead. I'm going to the lav." I said, "She's not dead. She's in a wheelchair with a broken heart. He's been having you on."

After a bit she comes out. "You're just saying all this." "The number's on the pad. Ring up. She's disabled is his wife. Has been for ten years. Their daughter looks after them. You're not the first. He's always doing it. One woman, it was going to be Barbados. Somebody spotted you together at Bolton Abbey. A well-wisher. Tenerife!"

Later on I took her a cup of tea. She'd been crying. She said, "I bought this little bedjacket." I said, "I'm sorry, Mam." She said, "He was right enough. What can you expect at my age? How old am I?" "Seventy-two." "That's another thing. I remembered with him. I don't remember with you." I said, "I'm sorry." She said, "You're not sorry. How are you sorry? You didn't like him." I said, "He wasn't good enough for you." She said, "I'm the best judge of that. He was natty, more than can be said for you." And starts crying again. I said, "I understand, Mam." She said, "You don't understand. How can you understand, you, you're not normal?" I said, "I'm going to bed."

In a bit she comes shouting outside the door. "You think you've got it over me, Graham Whittaker. Well, you haven't I've got it over you." I said, "Go back to bed." She said, "I know the kind of magazines you read." I said, "Chess. You'll catch cold." She said, "They never are chess. Chess with no clothes on. Chess in their birthday suits. That kind of chess. Chess men." I said, "Go to bed. And turn your blanket off."

Pause.

Next day she's right as rain. Forgotten it. Never mentions it anyway, except just as we're coming out of the house she says, "I do love you, Graham." I said, "I love you too." She said, "Anyway he had a hearing aid." She said, "What's on the agenda for today, then?" I said, "I thought we might have a little ride to Ripon." She said, "Oh yes, Ripon. That's nice, We could go to the cathedral. We like old buildings, don't we, you and me?"

She put her arm through mine.

The lights fade to blackout.

Curtain.

FURNITURE AND PROPERTY LIST

On stage: Bed
Bedside table. *On it:* cup of tea
Wardrobe
Two upright chairs
Armchair

LIGHTING PLOT

Practical fittings required: nil

Interior. The same scene throughout

To open: General interior lighting

Cue 1	**Graham**: "She put her arm through mine." *Fade lights*	(Page 6)
Cue 2	**Graham** stands down stage of downstage right chair *Bring up lights*	(Page 6)
Cue 3	**Graham** sits in the chair right *Fade lights, then bring them up when ready*	(Page 9)
Cue 4	**Graham**: "...that chapter was closed." *Fade lights*	(Page 11)
Cue 5	**Graham** sits and drinks tea *Bring up lights*	(Page 11)
Cue 6	**Graham** moves to the right of the wardrobe *Fade lights*	(Page 13)
Cue 7	**Graham** sits in the armchair *Bring up lights*	(Page 13)
Cue 8	**Graham**: "She put her arm through mine." *Fade lights to blackout*	(Page 15)

EFFECTS PLOT

Cue 1   Before the curtain rises   (Page 1)
        Music

Cue 2   Curtain rises   (Page 1)
        Fade music

Cue 3   **Graham**: "She put her arm through mine." (Page 6)
        Music

Cue 4   **Graham** stands down stage of the
           downstage right chair   (Page 6)
        Fade music

Cue 5   **Graham** "...in case there's nobody there."   (Page 9)
        Music

Cue 6   Lights come up on **Graham**   (Page 9)
        Fade music

Cue 7   **Graham**: "...that chapter was closed."   (Page 11)
        Music

Cue 8   **Graham** sits and drinks tea   (Page 11)
        Fade music

THIS
IS
NOT
THE
END

**Visit samuelfrench.co.uk
and discover the best
theatre bookshop
on the internet**

A vast range of plays
Acting and theatre books
Gifts